Presented by:

_____

To:

_____

Date:

_____

Occasion:

_____

Songs Out of Silence

"99 Words to Live By"

A series of fine gift books that presents inspirational words by renowned authors and captivating thinkers. Thought-provoking proverbs from many peoples and traditions complete each volume's collection.

"99 Words to Live By" explores topics that have moved and will continue to move people's hearts. Perfect for daily reflection as well as moments of relaxation.

Songs Out
of Silence

99 Sayings
by Jessica Powers

edited by

Robert F. Morneau

New City Press
Hyde Park, New York

Published in the United States by New City Press
202 Comforter Blvd., Hyde Park, NY 12538
©2010 New City Press

Cover design by Leandro De Leon

Library of Congress Cataloging-in-Publication Data:

A copy of the CIP data is available from the
Library of Congress

ISBN 978-1-56548-250-0 (hardcover)

Printed in the United States of America

Jessica Powers (1905-1988) entered the Carmel of the Mother of God in Milwaukee, Wisconsin, in 1941. She took the religious name Sister Miriam of the Holy Spirit. For forty-seven years, she lived a contemplative life of prayer and fasting, of community and sacrifice, indeed, a life of faith, hope, and love. Her Scotch-Irish background marked her with both humor and melancholy, but her heart was centered on the mystery of God.

God graced Jessica Powers with a poetic heart. Year after year, her words captured various aspects of our human journey: birth and death, love and fear, sin and grace, joy and sorrow. Jessica Powers was a "noticer"; few things escaped her attentive mind and heart. Graced with an agile pen, she was able to transpose life's experiences into verses that have enriched thousands of people's lives.

Most of the "sayings" of Jessica Powers in this volume come from *The*

Selected Poetry of Jessica Powers (Washington, D.C.: ICS Publications, 1999), which has gone through six reprintings since it was first published in 1989. The reader is encouraged to check out *The Selected Poetry* for the context of the "sayings."

We all stand in need of models and mentors, of witnesses of gospel living and wise guides. Although she would never have claimed this title, Jessica Powers is a mentor. Through her insights and creative writings, she has left us a legacy of wisdom that can sustain us on life's long pilgrimage. Though a cloistered contemplative, now deceased some twenty years, she continues to teach us many things about the ways of God and the wonders of God's world.

Robert F. Morneau

This Trackless Solitude

Deep in the soul the acres lie
of virgin lands, of sacred wood
where waits the Spirit. Each soul
   bears
this trackless solitude.

...

The soul that wanders, Spirit led,
becomes, in His transforming
   shade,
the secret that she was, in God,
before the world was made.

And Wilderness Rejoices

Earth keeps its seasons and its
  liturgy,
as should the soul. Oh, come,
  green summer, blur
these wastes and let my soul in
  song declare.
Who came by flesh and Who by fire
  to her.

God Is Today

God is the dawn, wakening earth
   to life;
the first morning ever,
shining with infinite innocence; a
   revelation
older than all beginning, younger
   than youth.
God is the noon, blinding the eye
   of the mind
with the blaze of truth.
God is the sunset, casting over
   creation
a color of glory
as He withdraws into mysteries of
   light.

Repairer of Fences

Whom do I love, O God, when I
  love Thee?
The great Undoer who has torn
  apart
the walls I built against a human
  heart,
the Mender who has sewn together
  the hedges
through which I broke when I went
  seeking ill,
the Love who follows and forgives
  me still.

God Is a Strange Lover

God is a strange lover; the story
   of His love is most surprising.
There is no proud queen in her
   cloth of gold; over and over again
there is only, deep in the soul, a
   poor disheveled woman weep-
   ing...
for us who have need of a picture
   and words: the Magdalen.

The Will of God

Listen, and tell your grief: But
  God is singing!
God sings through all creation with
  His will.
Save the negation of sin, all is His
  music,
even the notes that set their roots
  in ill
to flower in pity, pardon or sweet
  humbling.
Evil finds harshness of the rack
  and rod
in tunes where good finds tender-
  ness and glory.

The Kingdom of God

Not in the quiet arms, O sorrowful
   lover;
O fugitive, not in the dark on a
   pillow of breast;
hunt not under the lighted leaves
   for God, —
here is the sacred Guest.

There is a Tenant here.
Come home, roamer of earth, to
   this room and find
a timeless Heart under your own
   heart beating,
a Bird of beauty singing under
   your mind.

The Ledge of Light

God is a thousand acres to me now
of high sweet-smelling April and the flow
of windy light across a wide plateau.

Ah, but when love grows unitive I know
joy will upsoar, my heart sing, far more free,
having come home to God's infinity.

The Master Beggar

Worse than the poorest mendicant alive,
the pencil man, the blind man with his breath
of music shaming all who do not give,
are You to me, Jesus of Nazareth.

Must You take up Your post on every block
of every street? Do I have no release?
Is there no room of earth that I can lock
to Your sad face, Your pitiful whisper "Please"?

The First Pentecost

That was the day [Pentecost] when
   Fire came down from heaven,
inaugurating the first spring of love.
Blood melted in the frozen veins,
   and even
the least bird sang in the mind's
   inmost grove.
The seed sprang into flower, and
   over all
still do the multitudinous blossoms
   fall.

The Spirit's Name

But when at last you are alone
   with Him
deep in the soul and past the
   senses' choir,
Oh, give Him then that title which
   will place
His unpredictable breath upon your
   face:
O Dove, O Flame, O Water, Wind
   and Cloud!
(And here the creature wings go
   veering higher)
O love that lifts us wholly into God!

O Deifier.

Night of Storm

Where love has been
burns the great lantern of the Holy
   Ghost.
Here in His light, review your world
   of frost:
a drifting miracle! What had been
   night
reels with unending eucharists of
   light.

Come, South Wind

I am saying all day to Love who
  wakens love:
rise in the south and come!
Hurry me into springtime; hustle
  the winter
out of my sight; make dumb
the north wind's loud impertinence.
  Then plunge me
into my leafing and my blossoming,
and give me pasture, sweet and
  sudden pasture.
Where could the Shepherd bring
his flocks to graze? Where could
  they rest at noonday?
O south wind, listen to the woe I
  sing!
One whom I love is asking for the
  summer
from me, who still am distances
  from spring.

To Love with the Spirit

To live with the Spirit of God
   is to be a listener.
It is to keep the vigil of mystery,
earthless and still.
One leans to catch the stirring of
   the Spirit,
strange as the wind's will.

...

To live with the Spirit of God is to
   be a lover.
It is becoming love, and like to
   Him
toward Whom we strain with
   metaphors of creatures:
fire-sweep and water-rush and the
   wind's whim.

The Little Nation

Having no gift of strategy or arms,
no secret weapon and no walled
    defense,
I shall become a citizen of love,
that little nation with the blood-
    stained sod
where even the slain have power,
    the only country
that sends forth an ambassador to
    God.

Letter of Departure

We knew too much of the know-
    able dark world,
its secret and its sin,
too little of God. And now we rise
    to see
that even our pledges to humanity
were false, since love must out of
    Love begin.

My Heart Ran Forth

Back toward the house from which I deftly fled,
down neighbors' lanes, across my father's barley
my heart brought home its charity. It said:
love is a simple plant like a Creeping Charlie;
once it takes root its talent is to spread.

I Hold My Heart
As A Gourd

I hold my heart as a gourd ready
  to pour
upon all those who live.
Not that I see each one as come
  from God
and to my soul His representative,
but that God inhabits what He loves
and what His love sustains, and
  hence I see
in each soul that may brush
  against my soul
God Who looks out at me.

The Rock Too
High for Me

Though bathed in an immeasur-
   able forgiveness,
a blinding love that wakes the fur-
   thest trust,
yet I am Moses straining his eyes
   on Pisgah;
I am Job, stopping his mouth with
   ashes;
I am Jeremiah, face in the dust.

Come Is the
Love Song

Come is the love song of our
   race and Come
our basic word of individual woo-
   ing.
It lifts audacious arms of lowliness
to majesty's most amiable undo-
   ing,
to Godhood fleshed and cradled
   and made least.
It whispers through closed doors a
   hurry, hurry
to Tierce and fiery feast.

The Homecoming

The spirit, newly freed from earth,
is all amazed at the surprise
of her belonging; suddenly
as native to eternity
to see herself, to realize
the heritage that lets her be
at home where all this glory lies.

By naught foretold could she have
    guessed
such welcome home: the robe,
    the ring,
music, and endless banqueting,
these people hers; this place of
    rest
known, as of long remembering
herself a child of God and pressed
with warm endearments to His
    breast.

And In Her Morning

God is a light and genitor of
   light.
Yet for our weakness and our
   punishment
He hides Himself in midnights that
   prevent
all save the least awarenesses of
   Him.
We strain with dimmed eyes
   inward and perceive
no stir of what we clamored to
   believe.

Abraham

I love Abraham, that old weather-beaten
unwavering nomad; when God called to him,
no tender hand wedged time into his stay.
His faith erupted him into a way
far-off and strange. How many miles are there
from Ur to Haran? Where does Canaan lie,
or slow mysterious Egypt sit and wait?

In a Cloud of Angels

I walk in a cloud of angels.
God has a throne in the secret of
  my soul.
I move, encircled by light,
blinded by glowing faces,
lost and bewildered in the motion
  of wings,
stricken by music too sublime to
  bear.

Ministering Spirits

Never go anywhere without the
 angels
who watch God's face and listen
 to be sought.
Greater than you, yet they have
 joy to serve you.
Never go blundering through
 the jungle, thought,
without a clear-eyed one to part
 the branches,
shout snake or swamp-hole, cry
 a rock beware.
The angels of the Lord encamp
 around you
in any place you pitch your tents
 for prayer.

At Sunset

Color and light possess me. I am
  one
with stars and moonlight and the
  dying sun.

Siesta in Color

Near a glazed window drinking
   south and west
in thirst of sunlight in the early
   spring,
I with a sudden luck of illness take
magic siesta. I commune with
   color,
hobnob with rainbows on the
   coasts of slumber,
revisit prisms of long disregard.

O Full of Lilies

Easter to me my little sister is,
and I affirm her April's eminence.
No beauty of atoning penances
prevails on light as does her
innocence.

In Too Much Light

The Magi had one only star to
　follow,
a single sanctuary lamp hung low,
gold ornament in the astonished
　air.
I am confounded in this latter day;
I find stars everywhere.

Advent

I live my Advent in the womb of
    Mary.
And on one night when a great
    star swings free
from its high mooring and walks
    down the sky
to be the dot above the *Christus i,*
I shall be born of her by blessed
    grace.
I wait in Mary-darkness, faith's
    walled place,
with hope's expectance of nativity.

Counsel for Silence

Go without ceremony of departure
ture
and shade no subtlest word with
your farewell.
Let the air speak the mystery of
your absence,
and the discerning have their
minor feast
on savory possible or probable.

There Is a Homelessness

There is a homelessness, never to
    be clearly defined.
It is more than having no place
    of one's own, no bed or chair.
It is more than walking in a waste
    of wind,
or gleaning the crumbs where
    someone else has dined,
or taking a coin for food or clothes
    to wear.
The loan of things and the denial
    of things are possible to bear.

The Moment After Suffering

Time's cupped hand holds
no place so lenient, so calm as
   this,
the moment after suffering. It is
   like
a sunlit clearing after densest
   wood,
bright by antithesis.

Creature of God

That God stands tall, incompre-
    hensible,
infinite and immutable and free,
I know. Yet more I marvel that His
    call
trickles and thunders down
    through space to me....

The Soul That Cries to God

And He who redeems will use
for the soul
the full extent of its cargo:
the songs, the memory's trivia,
the sweet or acid tears,
the spoils or the debt of frightening
arrears.
Ingenious to save, in the end His
love
will put to divine advantage
the wisdom (if wisdom could be
the word) of the wasted years.

The Masses

I learned from God the ancient
    primal mother
whose hunger to create has
    brought forth these,
a multitude in lone nativities,
whose love conceived the number-
less, and none
but twos and thousands; and with
    Him I bear them
in separate tenderness, one by one.

If You Have Nothing

No gift is proper to a Deity;
no fruit is worthy for such power to
  bless.
If you have nothing, gather back
  your sigh,
and with your hands held high,
your heart held high,
lift up your emptiness!

Humility

Humility is to have place
deep in the secret of God's face

where one can know, past all sur-
  mises
that God's great will alone is wise,

where one is loved, where one can
  trust
a strength not circumscribed by
  dust.

On Reading Saint Peter
of Alcantara

How glorious, O soul, is this your journey!
Love is its end and love its plan and prod.
Set out then in the riches of your nothing.
Enter into the solitudes of God.

No One Can Stay

No one can stay
in any golden moment, and no
    more
will I let any trick of light betray
me to a house that is nothing but a
    door.

The Great Mystery

My uncle had one sober comment for
  ment for
all deaths. Well, he (or she)
has, he would say, solved the
  great mystery.
I tried as child to pierce the dark
  unknown
straining to reach the keyhole of
  that door,
massive and grave, through which
  one slips alone.

Draw Me: We Will Run

O God, my Hive, protect me as I come,
a laden bee bearing its treasure home.

The Tear in the Shade

I tore the new pale window shade
  with slightly
more than a half-inch tear.
I knew the Lady would be shocked
  to see
what I had done with such finality. I
went outside to lose my worry there.
Later when I came back into the
  room
it seemed that nothing but the tear
  was there.

There had been furniture, a rug,
  and pictures,
and on the table flowers in purple
  bloom.
It was amazing how they dwindled,
  dwindled,
and how the tear grew till it filled
  the room.

The Soul Is a Terrible Thing

Oh, at this mystery that lies
    within me — *This threshold standing* qeq
I walk indeed with trembling, or I
    stand
crying God's pities out of His right
    hand —
that I, so poor a creature, am so
    favored
with this too precious gift of soul,
    that I
bear in so undependable a vessel
this terrible, terrible thing they call
    a soul.

The House at Rest

How does one hush one's house,
each proud possessive wall, each
  sighing rafter,
the rooms made restless with re-
  membered laughter
or wounding echoes, the permis-
  sive doors,
the stairs that vacillate from up to
  down,
windows that bring in color and
  event
from countryside or town,
oppressive ceilings and complain-
  ing floors?

The Place of Splendor

No soul can view
its own geography; love does not
live
in places open and informative.

Wanderer

How did I ever come then to the
   light?
How did I ever, blind with self,
dis   cover
the small strict pathway to this
   shining place,
I who betrayed the truth over
and over, and let a tangle of dark
   woods surround me?
Simple the answer lies: down cliffs
   of pain,
through swamps and desert,
   thicket and terrain,
oh, Someone came and found me.

The Second Giving

God seeks a heart with bold and
    boundless hungers
that sees itself and earth as paltry
    stuff;
God loves a soul that cast down all
    He gave it
and stands and cries that it was
    not enough.

Track of the Mystic

There was a man went forth into the night
with a proud step. I saw his garments blowing;
I saw him reach the great cloud of unknowing.
He went in search of love, whose sign is light.
From the dark night of sense I saw him turn
into the deeper dark nights of the soul
where no least star marks a divine patrol.

There Shall Come
Forth a Shoot

I am waiting for a green shoot
to come out of my stump some
    morning
in this unseasonal springtime —
December's leaf and blossom,
    winter's bird.
Joy waits with me and I can feel its
    seepage
into my day and night.

…

Yet who am I to minimize the
    worth
of what a stump is likely to bring
    forth?

At Evening with a Child
(For Maureen)

We walk along a road
at the day's end, a little child and I,
and she points out a bird, a tree, a
    toad,
a stretch of colored sky.

She knows no single word
but "Ah" (with which all poems
    must commence,
at least in the heart's heart), and I
    am stirred
by her glad eloquence.

Water and Light

I see the light upon my sisters'
faces
lifted to God, world over. On these
stairs
glory and grace are cloudbursts
over me,
out of her [Madre Teresa's] soul
and theirs.
Have you seen water ever that got
tangled
with light and came alive and was
divine?
I drown in these torrents out of her
soul and theirs,
and (God forgive me) mine.

Prayer

Prayer is the trap-door out of sin.
Prayer is a mystic entering in
to secret places full of light.
It is a passage through the night.
Heaven is reached, the blessed
    say,
by prayer and by no other way.

The Sign of the Cross

The lovers of Christ lift out their hands to
the great gift of suffering.
For how could they seek to be warmed and clothed
and delicately fed,
to wallow in praise and to drink deep draughts
of an undeserved affection,
have castle for home and a silken couch for bed,
when He the worthy went forth, wounded and hated,
and grudged of even a place to lay His head?

The Heart Can
Set Its Boundaries

Only when God is passing by,
and is invited in to stay
is there a split of earth and sky.
Boundaries leap and rush away,

and wound and chaos come to be
where once a world lay, still and
    small.
But how else could Infinity
enter what is dimensional?

Christ Is My
Utmost Need

Christ is my utmost need.
I lift each breath, each beat for
   Him to bless,
knowing our language cannot
   overspeak
our frightening helplessness.

Here where proud morning walks
and we hang wreaths on power
   and self-command,
I cling with all my strength unto a
   nail-investigated hand.

Take Your Only Son

Hope may shout promise of reward unending
and faith buy bells to ring its glad   ness thrice,
but these do not preclude earth's tragic ending
and the heart shattered in its sacri-fice.

Not beside Abram does my story set me.
I built the altar, laid the wood for flame.
I stayed my sword as long as duty let me,
and then alas, alas, no angel came.

Return

I must come home again to sim-
   ple things:
robins and buttercups and bum-
   blebees,
laugh with the elves and try again
   to find
a leprechaun behind the hawthorn
   trees.

The Monastic Song

The theme is penance, poverty
the language.
And no luxuriant adverb must come
here
to swish its velvet robes, no ad-
jective
save one that is content to meet
and marry
with the obscure, the frugal, the
austere.
The theme is penance; this is
earth, not heaven.

Look at the Chickadee

I have this brief audacious word
  to say:
look at the chickadee,
that small perennial singer of the
  earth,
who makes the weed of a Decem-
  ber day
the pivot of his mirth.

Everything
Rushes, Rushes

The brisk blue morning whisked
  in with a thought:
everything in creation rushes,
  rushes
toward God — tall trees, small
  bushes,
quick birds and fish, the beetles
  round as naught,

eels in the water, deer on forest
  floor,
what sits in trees, what burrows
  underground,
what wriggles to declare life must
  abound,
and we, the spearhead that run on
  before....

Wisconsin Winter

When we send greetings on a
   snow-scene
card or gift at Christmas, will we
   not wonder whether
there might be more than wishful
   words to find:
a sunrise, maybe, for the inmost
   mind;
for deepest heart, some Arizona
   weather?

The Valley of
My Childhood

The creek was our joy; we pushed
  our naked toes
into its kissing clearness where the
  minnows
ran up the scale of silver in their
  flight.
The clam pretended not to be one
  of us
and drew his doorway tight.
Sometimes along the willowed
  shore we startled
the wary killdeer and wading crane.

The Cedar Tree

I clasp this thought: from all eternity
God who is good looked down upon this tree
white in the weighted air,
and of another cedar reckoned well.
He knew how much each tree, each twig could bear.
He counted every snowflake as it fell.

Bird at Daybreak

Here is a small bird cast as John
   the Baptist
who from my treetops is inspired
   to say:
I come from heaven to prepare the
   way.
Now in the east approach the feet
   of day.

Poet of a
Gentler Time

My words torment him with the
   prick of arrows.
Not soon, not ever will he under-
   stand
that love may learn the accent of
   the sparrows,
having no larks or nightingales at
   hand.

For a Silent Poet

Weep not that visit of a brief
   duration.
You are a guest yourself and you
   must know
that in you lie the instincts of
mi gration,
and where the bird went, one day
   you will go.

Robin at Dusk

Oh, that a song of mine could burn
the air with beauty so intense,
sung with a robin's unconcern
for any mortal audience!

Perhaps I shall learn presently
his secret when the shadows stir,
and I shall make one song and be
aware of but one Listener.

Birds

That God made birds is surely in
　His favor.
I write them as His courtesies of
　love.
Hidden in leaves, they offer me
　sweet savor
of lightsome music; when they
　streak above

my garden wall they brush my
　scene with color.
They are embroideries upon the
　grass.
I write the gayest stitched-in
　blossoms duller
than birds which change their
　patterns as I pass.

Doxology

God fills my being to the brim
with floods of His immensity.
I drown within a drop of Him
whose sea-bed is infinity.

Night of Storm

And now the soul is supplicant: O most
Wretched and blind, come home! Where love has been
Burns the great lantern of the Holy Ghost.
Here in His light, review your world of frost:
A drifting miracle! What had been night
Reels with unending eucharists of light.

Song of the
Immortal Soul

All You little birds of God that
sing and fly,
From you I hide this bright bird of
my breast;
For if you saw his far-winged jour-
neying,
Your flight might fail; your song
die unexpressed
If, listening at the stars, you heard
him sing.

Lo Spirito Santo

The Spirit of God
Is wind and water,
Fire and a bird.
It is energy shod;
Motion and matter,
One breath, one word.

To One Killed in War

And I know, as well as I know
    earth is not my mother
And my dust will leave her some
    day,
That the road of suffering runs
    farther than any other
Toward God. It was His chariot of
    life, His horses of love that ran
    this way.

To Francis Thompson

Pray God to halt me in my tracks
    this day
With that strange wisdom that you
    found so sweet:
We are of Love not hunters but the
    prey.

"Poetry — and prose — should have a certain discipline and restraints, don't you think? I'm inclined to write more than I should or the wrong thing. Was it Michelangelo who said that art (beauty) is cutting away the superfluous?"

(Letter: August, 1987)

76

"We thought spring had come, but winter is here again. We liked watching the wild geese go north again — so many flocks. We hear them honking and go to see. I was in admiration of the leader who struck out ahead, bearing the brunt of the wind, leading the flock in beautiful formation. They say that is what the world lacks today — strong leaders."

(Letter: March 17, 1988)

"When I was in New York, I recall, I could hardly bear the beautiful music that drifted up to me from a lower apartment. The sadness wasn't loneliness for people; I'm not sure it was even loneliness. Just too much beauty for the human heart to bear. That is why, I think, that solitude-and-silence is prescribed for our life (and in a measure for every life) because one seldom had deep thoughts and feelings amid distraction and noise."

(Letter: January 23, 1986)

"I think of a holy card that my aunt (who was a Sister of Mercy) gave me when I was a little girl — her jubilee card, with a beautiful angle on it and the words: "O sublime vow of obedience! How sweet are thy bonds to a soul that gives itself generously to God!" …

Anyway, I think that card influenced my life: a small hint of the beauty of holiness. We never know when or where a seed that is planted grows, do we? Some little thing can be a source of grace."

(Letter: October 31, 1986)

"There are graces in the writings of those not of our faith, aren't there? Sometimes lovely things that are lost. Beautiful things God scatters everywhere. As Walt Whitman said, (in other words), that God is tossing down love letters in the street and everywhere, if only we would watch out for them. I think I have come to see that even the contradictions and the crosses of life are His 'love letters.' "

(Letter: Ash Wednesday, 1987)

"I've begun to look for them [God's love letters] with a certain joy — signs that tell me that Jesus is near. The unexpected delay, the negative response, the inopportune caller, the gimmick that won't work, the nice food that got overcooked, the lack of something needed, the ballpoint pen that smudges, the mistake one can't undo — the list is endless. Not (I hope) that I concentrate on the unpleasant things but that they are little signs that I share in the life of Jesus."

(Ash Wednesday, 1987)

The Mountains of the Lord

I questioned innocence renewed
   by grace:
what did you see on hills beatified?
What voices heard you in the holy
   place?
With words of light the penitent
   replied:

Under the night's impenetrable
   cover
wherein I walked beset by many
   fears,
I saw the radiant face of Christ the
   Lover,
and it was wet with tears.

The Mystical Sparrow of Saint John of the Cross

Distantly pure and high, a mountain sparrow
is solitary in transfigured sky.
A ball of bird melodious with God
is lightsome in its love.
Not to dear mate or comrade do I cry
but to my own remote identity
who knows my spirit as divinely summoned
to gain that perch where no horizons lie.

But Not With Wine

O God of too much giving,
   whence is this
inebriation that possesses me,
that the staid road now wanders
   all amiss
and that the wind walks much too
   giddily,
clutching a bush for balance, or a
   tree?
How then can dignity and pride
   endure
with such inordinate mirth upon
   the land,
when steps and speech are some-
   what insecure
and the light heart is wholly out of
   hand?

The Garments of God

God sits on a chair of darkness in
   my soul.
He is God alone, supreme in His
   majesty.
I sit at His feet, a child in the dark
   beside Him;
my joy is aware of His glance and
   my sorrow is tempted
to nest on the thought that His
   face is turned from me.

This Is a Beautiful Time

This is a beautiful time, this last
   age, the age of
the Holy Spirit.
This is the long-awaited day of His
   reign in our
souls through grace.
He is crying to every soul that is
   walled:
Open to Me, My spouse, My sister.
And once inside, He is calling again:
Come to Me here in this secret
   place.
Oh, hear Him tonight crying all
   over the world
a last desperate summons of love
   to a dying race.

Shining Quarry

Since the luminous great wings
   of wonder stirred
over me in the twilight I have known
the Holy Spirit is the Poet's Bird.

Since in a wilderness I wandered
   near
a shining stag, this wisdom is my
   own:
the Holy Spirit is the Hunter's Deer.

And in the dark in all enchanted
   lands
I know the Spirit is that Burning
   Bush
toward which the artist gropes with
   outstretched hands.

The Spirit's Name

Dove is the name of Him and so
  is Flame,
and Love can push aside all eager
  symbols
to be His peerless and His proper
  name.
And Wind and Water, even Cloud
  will do,
if it is heart that has the interview.

The Flower of Love

Blessed are they who stand upon
   their vow
and are insistent
that love in this bleak here, this
   barren now
become existent.

Blessed are they who battle jest
   and scorn
to keep love growing
from embryo immaculately born
to blossom showing.

I Would Define My Love

How can a man in love sit and
stare?
O people of earth, if I am not with
you, running and crying,
it is that I am paging hurriedly
through wordless volumes of reality
to find what love has indicated
there.
I would define my love in some in-
credible penance
of which no impotent language is
aware.

The Pool of God

I pray to hollow out my earth and
be
filled with these waters of trans-
parency.
I think that one could die of this
desire,
seeing oneself dry earth or stub-
born sod.
Oh, to become a pure pool like the
Virgin,
water that lost the semblances of
water
and was a sky like God.

Beauty, Too, Seeks Surrender

God takes by love what yields to
   love,
then pours a glowing allness
past the demolished walls and
   towers
into the spirit's smallness.

God's beauty, too, surrender seeks
and takes in the will's lull
whatever lets itself be changed
into the beautiful.

Green Is the Season

Green is the season after Pentecost.
The Holy Ghost in an abstracted
   place
spreads out the languid summer
   of His peace,
unrolls His hot July.
O leaves of love, O chlorophyll of
   grace.

Israel Again

When will you learn, O witless
    Israel,
that he who clings to God in his
    distress
wins with the weapons of his
    nothingness?

This May Explain

The door to God, the door to any grace
is very little, very ordinary.
Those must remember who would gain the place
this rule that does not vary:
all truth, all love are by humiliation
guarded, as One has testified before.
This may explain why the serf finds salvation,
and kings and scholars pass the little door.

The Monk at Quadragesima

Come, death.
Walk in this season of your grim
    renown.
Come, let me have my bouts with
    you, knave
who tracked my Master down.

…

For certainly I know
that in our sharp encounter well I
    fare.
With you as guest beside me all is
    gain.
You slay me, death, but then I rise
    to live
and you yourself are slain.

Suffering

All that day long I spent the hours
    with suffering.
I woke to find her sitting by my
    bed.
She stalked my footsteps while
    time slowed to timeless,
tortured my sight, came close in
    what was said.

She asked no more than that,
    beneath unwelcome,
I might be mindful of her grant of
    grace.
I still can smile, amused, when I
    remember
how I surprised her when I kissed
    her face.

Obscurity

Obscurity becomes the final
　　peace.
The hidden then are the elect, the
　　free.
They leave our garish noon and
　　find release
in evening's gift of anonymity.

Enclosure

Gypsy by nature, how can I en dure it —
this small strict space, this mea ger patch of sky?
What madness once possessed me to procure it?
And deed it to myself until I die?

What could the wise Teresa have been thinking
to set these bounds on even my little love?
This walling, barring, minimizing, shrinking —
how could her great Castilian heart approve?

Sources

(The numbers refer to the selection number in the present book, followed by the page number in the cited work.)

The Selected Poetry of Jessica Powers
(Washington, D.C.: ICS Publications, 1999).
All copyrights, Carmelite Monastery, Pewaukee, WI.
Used with permission.

1:6; 2:7; 3:13; 4:14; 5:16; 6:19; 7:20; 8:22; 9:23;
10:25; 11:35; 12:36; 13:37; 14:38; 15:39;
16:43; 17:45; 18:46; 19:47; 20:49; 21:53;
22:64; 23:66; 24:68; 25:70; 26:74; 27:76;
28:78; 29:79; 30:81; 31:85; 32:86; 33:87;
34:88; 35:89; 36:90; 37:91; 38:92; 39:96;
40:98; 41:100; 42:116; 43:118; 44:121; 45:122;
46:123; 47:124; 48:133; 49:135; 50:139;
51:140; 52:141; 53:144; 54:150; 55:151;
56:152; 57:153; 58:157; 59:159; 60:162;
61:163; 62:164; 63:169; 64:176; 65:180;
66:185; 67:186; 68:187; 69:188; 70:191; 82:8;
83:11; 84:17 85:21; 86:27; 87:30; 88:35; 89:41;
90:50; 91:63; 92:72; 93:83; 94:93; 95:95;
96:105; 97:106; 98:108; 99:128

Jessica Powers, *The Lantern Burns*
(New York: The Monastery Press, Copyright 1939).
Used with permission.

71:3; 72:12; 73:16; 74:25; 75:47

Unpublished Letters

76: Letter, August 1987; 77: Letter, March 17
1988; 78: Letter, January 23 1986; 79: Letter,
October 31 1986; 80: Letter, Ash Wednesday
1987; 81: Letter, Ash Wednesday 1987